Lean, Innovation and The Spirit of Enterprise

DEVSENA MISHRA

*To my elder sister Dr. Gargi Mishra and her husband Mr. Siddharth,
thank you so much for your love and support...*

PREFACE

I consider Automation, Computer, Internet, Telephone, Mobile etc. as breakthrough Innovations. These innovations have shaped the world economy. Mr. George Gilder in 'The Spirit of Enterprise' said "Entrepreneurs are innovators who evoke demand. They are makers of markets, creators of capital, developers of opportunity and producers of new technology. They seek the unique product, the marketing breakthrough, the startling new feature or the novel design. They change technical frontiers and reshape public desires. They create wealth and employment. They take exception to the received view that companies should market-led. They lead the market." I think the world economy is needed a new push again. For some time now a gap has been created and this is a perfect time for something great to happen.

Today's entrepreneurs are quite smart, their approach is 'Lean', they are living in a much better atmosphere, and above all, they have a rich source of experience of earlier entrepreneurs. The combination of all these factors have reduced the duration of the gap between innovations, now 5-10 years are enough to create something that can push the whole economy and it's a good sign.

As an IT professional I can feel the upheaval of the world economy, and the gap that is being created…this book is a compilation of my short notes on these trends. This book starts with a brush-up of popular Lean process improvement tools. In the second chapter, I have shared the concept of "Lean Innovation Approach" because I observed that existing innovation efforts of some enterprises lack two things: the vision and spirit of the entrepreneur and lean management. The third chapter is an overview of 'Knowledge and Innovation economy', the current economic trend. Last three chapters of this book cover the case study of those countries that are best examples of the spirit of enterprise- Israel, Singapore and India. Israel is a remarkable example of technological innovations; Singapore is one of the largest financial hub and India has emerged as a bright spot of hope for the world economy. I believe in the growth of a country, it is spirit and passion that matters, the leaders of these three countries have inspired their citizen through their actions and the results are phenomenal…

Table of Contents

Overview of Process Improvement Frameworks

Management and Business frameworks are time-tested best practices that we apply in our work for the betterment of processes. There are several frameworks exist for each stage of business. Transformations in Technology and business Innovation trends have created an environment of healthy and open competition. In each and every stage of business, continuous improvement of the process is a must. Process improvement helps a business to match its capabilities with the demand and trends of the market. When an organization tries to create a culture of innovation within an organization, identification of all those processes is needed that are creating hurdle or too rigid to incorporate innovation. I believe that process improvement is itself a kind of innovation. Smoother running processes bring self-motivation and self-motivation brings excellence. In this chapter, we will see an overview of popular process improvement frameworks/tools…

Lean Management- Lean Management is an effective management approach. The key focus of Lean is identification and elimination of wasteful actions. This approach is derived from Lean Manufacturing practices that are developed by Toyota. If a process is not working well or not working as per standards and actual cause of the problem is not known, we can apply a systematic approach and certain lean tools to analyze the situation and can improve the process. The lean methodology has specified that there are typically 8 types of possible waste (8th waste underutilization of skills was added later) called WORMPITS- Waiting, Over-Production, Rework, Motion, Over-Processing, Inventory, Transportation and Underutilization of Skills). Lean Management can improve the efficiency and pace of existing processes, earlier I have written an article 'Application of lean management in professional life and organizational growth' that describes how to apply lean in professional life and for organizational growth. I believe that as a part of continuous process improvement, the organization needs to continuously analyze what processes/policies can be a good candidate for lean management.

These days our government is also applying lean management as our Prime Minister Mr. Modi has said, his team is trying to eliminate all those policies/laws that are creating waste in the government system. I believe Lean approach is needed in India for enabling Ease of Doing Business too. Lean approach is a symbol of seriousness toward process excellence.

Lean Tools:

Kaizen- It is one of the popular Lean Tool that helps in improving the process. Kaizen (a Japanese word that means improvement) emphasizes that one should first analyze the current state of work or situation, and then visualize the ideal situation and make improvements accordingly; to perform these activities PDCA (plan, do, check, act) cycle can be implemented. Kaizen helps in minimizing the labor and space requirements, increases flexibility, quality, responsiveness and boosts employee morale. Kaizen is applicable in those situations when a solution of a problem is simple and can be implemented using a team-based approach. In a Kaizen event which is usually 3-5 days long, teams gather and brainstorms the solution of a problem.

8 wastes in Lean- The Main concept of lean is streamlining of processes through identification and elimination of waste activities/processes/sub-processes. Waste is any activity that is not creating any value and its existence in the process flow is not solving any purpose. There are eight types of waste: Waiting, Over-Production, Rework, Motion, Over-Processing, Inventory, Transportation and Underutilization of Skills.

Pull Systems- Pull system as it sounds is based on a concept that manufacturing should be planned according to the actual information that is coming from the market or customer instead of any forecast or previous records. It is different from traditional 'push' concept of keep making items without knowing whether it is needed in downstream or not. Push and Pull both are inventory management system and which one to choose depends on a number of factors. There are some organizations that use 'push-pull strategy' which combines the best of both. This approach focuses on stable supply chain and elimination/reduction of wastes. The popular Kanban system is also inspired from the Pull System. In Kanban system inventory is managed by signals called 'Kanban cards' to notify about the status of inventory, parts or products. Kanban is a demand driven, Just in Time manufacturing system. In software development process, a hybrid of Scrum and Kanban called 'Scrumban' is becoming popular too.

Continuous Flow- To eliminate waste from the production line by reducing queue time and to reduce overall cycle time we can use Continuous flow approach. In a typical discrete manufacturing system, batches of product units are routed from one process to other where each process adds some value to the product. In a batch, each unit has to wait for the rest of the batch to complete and this wait time depends on the size of the batch, the larger the batch, the longer the wait time. In a Continuous Flow process, a single unit travels each stage of production sequentially. This single piece flow minimizes waiting time waste, reduces cost and establishes an error free production flow and balanced production line.

5S- This lean tool can be applied to create and maintain an organized, clean and high-performance work area. **The 5S's are Sort, Stabilize, Shine, Standardize, and Sustain.** It's a systematic way to improve process and workplace.

Standard Work- To streamline a process of production or service delivery, we can define standard steps to be followed by the team as a best practice. The use of standard work reduces process variations and enhances the quality of work. The process of defining standard work is a step toward process improvement, it forms a baseline for improvement. From my experience of working with different service organizations, I would say it is quite an effective approach and a must for customer facing operations. While defining standard work is important for a product company, a service organization cannot afford its executives to apply their personal approach to deal with customer issues too, there should be a standard way of dealing to be followed by each executive. Standard work improves the customer experience and sets high standards of delivery. Refinement of defined standard work steps based on customer feedback and trends in the market is also needed.

Poka-Yoke (Mistake Proofing) - Detection and prevention are the goals of Poka-Yoke, this lean technique is used for mistake proofing operation. There are three approaches to Poka-Yoke- Warning, Auto Correction, and Shutdown. Mistake proofing approach should warn the user/operator, correct the process automatically or shut down the process to prevent any damage.

Lean-TPM (Total Productive Maintenance) - As the name indicates this lean tool's focus is to improve the productivity of the System with the help of all employees at all levels. Lean TPM emphasizes equipment effectiveness and safety of employees. Its main objective is identification, prioritization, and elimination of all those factors that are causing delays and breakdowns in a manufacturing process and keeping all resources in good working condition to avoid breakdowns and delays. TPM assigns the responsibility for maintenance to the same people who operate that equipment, which makes the people familiar with the machine. Eight Pillars of TPM are Focused Improvement, Autonomous maintenance, Planned Maintenance, Quality Maintenance, Cost Deployment, Early Equipment Management, Training and Education and Safety, Health & Environment.

Hoshin Kanri Management- A team with unclear objectives and inconsistent direction cannot achieve its goals. The goal of management should be to align the goals of individuals with the goals of the organization. It is necessary that everyone understands and feel linked to the vision of the organization. I observed that typically in an organization everyone receives the emails and news updates about top management strategies but only a few employees are used to familiar with the vision and strategy of their organization. The Hoshin Kanri Management is a systematic approach of aligning planning and execution at all levels of management. This approach provides a focus and tries to drive everyone toward strategic goals. I believe KPIs plays an important role here and a good amount of thought should be given to KPI design. For Hoshin Kanri implementation, it is necessary that once strategic plan from top management is prepared, middle management should develop their tactics to implement that plan. A regular review should be done to check the effectiveness of applied tactics and adjustment should be made based on the findings of the reviews.

Six Sigma- It is an organizational approach toward process excellence. Six Sigma tools help to improve the business processes and capability of an organization. A process could be product or service process and it can be external or internal. The word Six Sigma is derived from statistical terminology where Sigma stands for Standard Deviation, as per Six Sigma Standard a product process's defective rate can be only 3.4 defects per million units. Six Sigma not only talks about product quality but also about improvement in service delivery. There are two approaches to process improvement: DMADV- for new processes and DMAIC- for existing processes. Let's take a look:

Six Sigma DMADV (Define, Measure, Analyze, Design, Verify) - DMADV process is used at the time of defining a new process. If an organization wants its processes to be streamlined as per the six sigma standards, a DMADV approach can be applied for the designing of new processes. A DMADV process consists of following steps: Define, Measure, Analyze, Design, and Verify.

Six Sigma DMAIC (Define, Measure, Analyze, Improve, Control) - To assess, improve and control the existing processes, DMAIC approach can be applied. It is needed when an organization aims to improve its existing processes as per the Six Sigma standards. A DMAIC process steps are Define, Measure, Analyze, Improve, and Control.

Balanced Scorecard- Financial Measures of an organization are good indicators of its performance but to assess whether the organization is leading in the right direction or not, some other measures are needed, balanced scorecard provides a way to measure much better and comprehensive parameters. It's a management system that helps an organization to set and track its business objectives. Balanced Scorecard provides four legs to cover different business perspectives. These are Customer Scorecard, Financial Scorecard, Internal Business Process Scorecard and knowledge, Education and Growth Scorecard.

Agile- I consider Agile as a process improvement framework for software development process. Agile principles are inspired by Lean methodology. The agile approach in software development process helps in eliminating waste activities; developing software in small incremental steps helps in identifying defects earlier and improves customer satisfaction that comes with the quality. Agile methods and engineering practices streamlined the development process and enhance the quality/stability of the code. I have written a book 'A Guide to Scrum Developer' on agile engineering practices and methods, it is available on Amazon.

To conclude I would say that Lean and other process improvement tools really helps and provides a systematic approach to product and service delivery, and at the same time, these tools have an inherent element of customization. This does not mean making changes in the fundamental framework, but it does mean adjusting existing processes to fit and to make people feel comfortable about it. I always advocate the need for customization and creativity because it is necessary to remember that A Tool or Framework should not become a hurdle or waste in itself.

Lean Innovation Approach

Innovation and entrepreneurship are necessary elements of the innovation economy. Mr. George Gilder in his book 'Knowledge and Power' said "economic growth is driven by unpredictable human actions and creativity. Entrepreneurs create information where none existed before. Entrepreneurs have the most knowledge about the circumstances surrounding their businesses. Entrepreneurial activity is devoted to the creation of new goods and services and precisely because it is surprising, it cannot be planned or demanded by governments or even by customers."

As per the recent finding of Capgemini Consulting Report 52% of Fortune 500 companies have merged, been acquired or gone bankrupt since 2000. R&D investments are increasing but R&D returns decreasing. In 2014, around US$1.6 trillion was spent on R&D globally, despite this significant investment, the results are falling short. In consumer goods, for example, research shows that more than 85% of new products fail and only 5% of R&D staff feels highly motivated to innovate. (Source: The Innovation Game: Why and How Businesses are investing in Innovation Centers for more detail visit- https://www.capgemini-consulting.com/the-innovation-game)

Companies are building innovation centers/teams in the form of In-House Innovation labs, university residence, community anchor, and innovation outpost, launching accelerator programs, running Hackathons and encouraging their employees to take entrepreneurial/ intrapreneurial initiatives. In an article that is published in Harvard Business Review, Scott Kirsner has shared some interesting metrics that senior innovation executives are using: Revenue generated by new products, Number of projects in the innovation pipeline, Stage-gate specific metrics i.e. projects moving from one stage to the next, P&L impact or other financial impact and Number of ideas generated.

These metrics cannot satisfy the leadership vision of an organization! To sum up, the innovative ideas generated out of these events are good for the betterment of a process or a product feature but when it comes to contributing to the larger vision of the organization and economic growth, the C-level executives have to play their part because they are capable in separating signal from the noise. I observed that the role of leadership and accountability is missing in these existing innovation strategies. Innovation should be a top-down approach.

Lean Innovation Approach

Here I would like to quote the equation given by Mr. George Gilder 'Money = Time, Knowledge = Wealth, Learning = Growth '.

The need is to manage the most precious and scarce resource 'Time' carefully. Why lean? Because the existing innovation approach has become fat and we need to lose this excess fat…involving employees and customers in the innovation process is fashionable but there is a need to ensure that such activities will not create any waste and stay aligned with the business objectives.

I observed existing innovation strategies carefully and I found that the element of traditional leadership is missing. Senior executives need to recall their traditional role of a creative agent of change to bring 'creative surprises' in the innovation economy.

We can visualize this approach in two steps:

1. C-Level brainstorming- C-Level executives should sit together once in every six months to brainstorm innovation strategy of the organization. If needed, they can perform some sort of Hackathon too; the idea is that when these executives will discuss innovation, something fresh and huge will come up. This process will set the vision and direction for the next six months.

2. Mid-Management Accountability- Innovation projects leaders should ensure that everyone understands the innovation strategy and vision and they should remain accountable for this. Aligning project activities with innovation strategy and identification/elimination of waste in these activities should be their primary goals.

Here I'm sharing an example that shows how Zukerberg is playing his part in the innovation events at Facebook. It is necessary that senior leadership should provide confidence, direction and vision to the innovation process. Delegating this task to someone else is not a good idea.

Facebook Hack 50- Facebook Hack 50, Zuckerberg set the direction by saying "The idea today is to focus on applications of AI, the idea that there are so many new technologies that are getting built around pattern matching...image recognition, face recognition, speech, and language, All of these are different areas of AI and pattern matching, and we think we're really at the beginning of this, which is why we have such a big focus on this as a company".

Every year, the Facebook CEO announces a personal challenge, and this year, he has set out to build himself an AI system capable of running his house, a kind of household butler. Zuckerberg said "The idea isn't that you're going to build something in one day that is fully formed that you can then go ship. That, I don't think, is the way the world works. But what you can do is, instead of having these abstract debates about whether something is a good idea, you can put something down in code, and a lot of the debates that you might have about, 'Oh, is this interaction going to work or be good enough to be a viable thing?'—you can show that that's the case in a day. The ideas people come up with at hackathons influence the product roadmap that all the teams have at the company, and it ends up being how we incorporate a very large percent of what we build at the company" [1]. (Read more at: http://www.fastcompany.com/3056018/exclusive-inside-facebooks-ai-hackathon)

I think this is a perfect approach where direction and vision are given by the chief executive so that teams work in a right direction and stay aligned. The push for the innovation that will decide the direction for the organization should come from the top. The teams should always be encouraged to use creativity and innovative ideas in their projects and for improving the product features as much as possible.

Also, there are several intra-organization chambers and c-level executive groups/bodies exist, these existing platforms can help in scaling the Lean Innovation Approach at the country level.

Knowledge and Innovation Economy

In today's knowledge-based economy, the accumulation of knowledge drives growth. The author of the book "The Way the World Works" Mr. Jude Wanniski has once said, "Growth comes not from dollars in people's pockets but from ideas in their heads". The knowledge and innovation drives the 21st century economy. According to a report from Asian Development Bank (ADB), India, with its youthful population and thriving information and communication technology (ICT) industry, can become a leading knowledge-driven economy. The leadership of India is promoting a culture of knowledge and innovation through its ambitious programs like Make in India, Digital India, and Startup India. In 2014-15, India contributed 12.5 per cent of global growth. Prime Minister Shri Narendra Modi used to say that "India should become a digital India, which is a knowledge-based society and economy. Our market should become a knowledge market where every seller and buyer knows everything, and the workers in every sector are knowledge workers."

Knowledge, Innovation, and growth are interlinked. Knowledge drives Innovation and Innovation brings growth. As described by Mr. George Gilder "Whenever a company launches a new product it's really testing an idea; and if the idea succeeds, if it's supported in the marketplace, the knowledge inhering in that idea is incarnate in the economy. That is how growth occurs. It's a process of learning."

Innovation economy is a growing economic theory that emphasizes entrepreneurship and innovation. In Innovation economy technology, knowledge, entrepreneurship and innovation are seen as primary driving forces. This theory says that 'central goal of economic policy should be to encourage higher productivity through greater innovation and markets relying on input resources and price signals alone will not always be as effective in spurring higher productivity, and thereby economic growth. This is in contrast to neoclassical economics and Keynesian economics'. Mr. Joseph Schumpeter introduced innovation economics in his 1942 book Capitalism, Socialism, and Democracy. Schumpeter argued that creative destruction is crucial to capitalism [2]. (Source: Wikipedia)

Mr. George Gilder in his book 'Knowledge and Power' criticizes existing economic theories for not giving importance to innovation and entrepreneurship, he believes that economic growth is driven by unpredictable human actions and creativity and entrepreneurs are creative agents of change. Here I would like to quote his statement from Israel Test book "The most precious resource in the world economy is human genius". Futurist like Mr. Gilder plays an important role in creating a positive environment for innovation and entrepreneurship. I see Innovation economy as a natural transition. In the current environment, innovation has become one of the necessary elements for survival. As per the Bloomberg Innovation Index 2016 for fifty most innovative economies, South Korea tops the rank, while Singapore is at number six and Israel is at number 11. This index has included a number of parameters. Whatever these numbers speaks, Israel and Singapore have a good track record of technological innovations, these countries have challenged the classic economic models and there is a lot that other countries can learn from them. While in this ranking India is at number 45, I believe our current leadership's vision is bringing a fresh atmosphere of innovation in our country and its results will surprise the world.

India and Innovation Economy- India is an emerging innovation economy, our current government's initiatives are encouraging and promoting a culture of innovation and entrepreneurship. Prime Minister Mr. Narendra Modi is the strong supporter of technological innovation and entrepreneurship and he considers it as the most necessary element for India's economic growth. Our government's three major programs Digital India, Make in India and Startup India are designed to promote and support innovation. I have discussed all this in chapter 'India: An Emerging Innovation Economy'.

The mindset of a country's leadership is crucial for the growth of the economy. Next three chapters are dedicated to those countries that are an example of the spirit of enterprise- Israel, Singapore and an emerging hope 'India'. The leaders of these countries have turned unfavorable business innovation situations into favorable and set an example for others.

Israel – Case Study

Israel is a leader in research and technological creativity. Its accomplishments in the field of innovation and technologies are remarkable. As per the Bloomberg 2015 innovation index, Israel is the world's fifth-most innovative country and second in GDP expenditure on R&D. Since its establishment in 1948, Innovation is an important element of Israel's policy.

Let's take a look at some major factors that make Israel an example of entrepreneurial spirit:

Research and Development- Israel's technological researches in significant fields like computer technology, alternative technology, water treatment, agriculture, and communication are world known. The percentage of Israelis engaged in scientific and technological inquiry, and the amount spent on research and development (R&D) in relation to gross domestic product (GDP), is the second highest in the world. Since 2000, Israel has been a member of EUREKA, the pan-European research and development funding and coordination organization.

Israel's Office of the Chief Scientist (OCS) that comes under Ministry of Industry, Trade and Labor is responsible for executing the government policies that are related to industrial R&D support. The Government of Israel has signed agreements and created funds with other countries to support and promote industrial R&D cooperation [3]. (For more information visit: OCS Website)

Key International Research Bodies are:

MATIMOP-Israeli Industry Center For R&D, Bi-National Funds- Bi-national fund model to support cooperative projects with other nations, BIRD (Bi-National Industrial R&D)- American Israeli Foundation, BRITECH - Britain-Israel Industrial R&D Foundation, CIIRDF - Canada-Israel Industrial R&D Foundation, KORIL-RDF - Korea-Israel Industrial R&D Foundation, SIIRD - Singapore-Israel Industrial R&D Foundation, US-Israel Science & Technology Commission, IRC - Innovation Relay Centers.

Israel Governments Key initiatives to encourage technological and industrial research are:

Technological Incubators: The Technological Incubators program was introduced at the beginning of the 90s, since then the program has been open to all Israeli entrepreneurs. The technological Incubator program provides entrepreneurs following benefits: R&D grant, R&D infrastructure, Business guidance and Administrative assistance.

Pre-seed Fund- the TNUFA Program- TNUFA assists individual entrepreneur and start-up companies during the pre-seed stage.

Seed Fund - the HEZNEK Program- This program mobilizes funds for the establishment of start-up companies.

The MAGNET Program- MAGNET program promotes new technologies via cooperative venture between the industry and leading academic scientific research institutions in the field. This program provides a grant of up to 66% of approved budget.

MINI-MAGNET (MAGNETON) Program- Within the MAGNET umbrella, Mini-Magnet promotes technology transfer from academia to industry.

NOFAR Program- NOFAR comes under MAGNET program supports biotechnology projects.

(Read in detail from http://www.moit.gov.il/NR/rdonlyres/CD3AF19B-2619-415B-B2F4-B747101C5202/0/TheIntellectualCapital3550.pdf)

Israel has seven research universities: Bar-Ilan University, Ben-Gurion University of the Negev, the University of Haifa, Hebrew University of Jerusalem, the Technion – Israel Institute of Technology, Tel Aviv University and the Weizmann Institute of Science, Rehovot.

Other scientific research institutions include the Volcani Institute of Agricultural Research in Beit Dagan, the Israel Institute for Biological Research and the Soreq Nuclear Research Center. The Ben-Gurion National Solar Energy Center at Sde Boker is an alternative energy research institute established in 1987 by the Ministry of National Infrastructures to study alternative and clean energy technologies. Israeli universities are ranked among the top 50 academic institutions in the world in the following scientific disciplines: in chemistry (Technion), in computer science (Weizmann Institute of Science, Technion, Hebrew University, Tel Aviv University), in mathematics and natural sciences (Hebrew University, Technion) and in engineering (Technion).

There are over 250 foreign R&D Centers in Israel, here is a list of multinationals with R&D Centers in Israel

(Source of facts: Wikipedia and moit.gov.il)

Agricultural research

Agricultural innovations of Israel are remarkable. Israel has shown that how geniuses can turn unfavorable situations into favorable. Israel where more than half of the land is desert has established itself as a leader in advanced agriculture technologies. Israel not only produces its own food but also exports $1.3 billion worth of agricultural produce annually.

Israel's scientists, consultants, farmers and agriculture-related industries cooperate in Agriculture Research activities. Agricultural Research Organization (ARO), widely known as the Volcani Institute is responsible for operating research operations in the country. The Faculty of Agriculture of the Hebrew University of Jerusalem, Tel Aviv University, Bar Ilan University, Ben Gurion University of the Negev and the Weizmann Institute of Science also engage in agricultural research.

Agriculture Research Organization (ARO) – ARO's goal is to develop Israeli agriculture economy. ARO's six institutes are responsible for Plant Sciences, Animal Science, Plant Protection, Soil, Water and Environmental Sciences, Agricultural Engineering, and Postharvest and Food Sciences. ARO operates four research stations, in various parts of the country, and serves as a testing center for agricultural produce and equipment. Israel's Gene Bank for Agricultural Crops is also located on the ARO Volcani Center campus. ARO provides direct and cooperative technical assistance to developing countries with various national, regional, international and non-governmental agencies.

(Source of facts: http://www.agri.gov.il)

Israel's Key Agricultural Innovations [4]:

Drip irrigation- Israeli water engineer Simcha Blass, discovered that a slow and balanced drip led to remarkable growth. In 1965 Simcha Blass started a company called Netafim that provides drip and micro irrigation products for agriculture, greenhouse, landscape and mining applications. Israel's drip irrigation techniques helped several farming families in Senegal to reap crops three times a year, even on infertile land. The Israeli drip irrigation system, called Tipa ("Drop") includes a cement reservoir, a water pump (that can be operated by hand, solar power pump or diesel generator) and plastic irrigation pipes. This technique uses gravity that sends the water right to the roots of the plants, minimizing evaporation, soil leaching and the need for high volumes of pesticides and fertilizers [4].

Grain cocoons- Grain Cocoons is designed for toxic-free fumigation and safe storage of agricultural commodities. The huge bags, invented by international food technology consultant Prof. Shlomo Navarro, keep both water and air out. Traditional storage baskets or bags are not effective in keeping hungry bugs and micro-contaminants out. Grain Cocoon is an effective solution to keep insect, water, and water vapor penetration into the contents [4].

Biological pest control- Israeli company called Bio-Bee breeds beneficial insects and mites for biological pest control and bumblebees for natural pollination in greenhouses and open fields. Bio-Bee products have enabled sweet-pepper farmers to reduce the use of chemical pesticides by 75 percent. Bio-Bee exports eight different species of biological control agents, plus pollinating bumblebees, to 32 nations from Japan to Chile [4].

Dairy farming- Israeli Dairy Firms like Afimilk (formerly known as SAE Afikim) and SCR Precise Dairy Farming provides advanced systems for herd management, monitoring and feeding worldwide. Afimilk's notable inventions are: The first electronic milk meter, which measures how many liters of milk a cow has produced, the pedometer, which counts the number of steps a cow takes, indicating the right time for insemination, AfiFarm, a milking and dairy herd management software program, AfiAct, a fertility detection system and AfiLab, a device that analyses the components of the milk and detects bacteria.

SCR dairy has played a significant role in the development of innovative technological solutions for the worldwide dairy industry. During its first 20 years of operations, the company focused on developing electro-mechanical devices for dairy farms, pulsators, and automatic detachers. Over the last 10 years, SCR firmly established its place amongst dairy farmers, leading the industry with advanced cow monitoring solutions based on activity and rumination sensors. SCR is known for its heat detection tag technology, data flow management software for monitoring data, rumination monitoring tag and other advanced and innovative cow monitoring solutions.

AKOL- Agricultural Knowledge On-Line (AKOL) provides a software that help producers grow fruits and vegetables, raise poultry and dairy cows, manage vineyards and make olive oil. AKOL is hosted in IBM cloud, provides Israeli experts advice to farmers from anywhere in the world. Hundreds of thousands of farmers can obtain tailor-made solutions, arrange group purchases of supplies and communicate with colleagues [4].

Desert Potatoes - Hebrew University's Prof. David Levy developed strains of potatoes that flourish in hot, dry climates, and can be irrigated by saline water sources. His development will have a huge impact on potato production in hot, desert regions like the Middle East, where temperatures are scorching, and water resources scarce [4].

Crop protection- Two years ago, Hebrew University's tech transfer company teamed with ADAMA Agricultural Solutions Ltd. (formerly Makhteshim Agan Industries Ltd.) an Israeli manufacturer and distributor of branded off-patent crop protection products including herbicides, insecticides, and fungicides. The Israeli approach incorporates herbicides into micelles or vesicles, which are absorbed onto negatively charged clay minerals to enable a slow and controlled release, reducing leaching to deeper soil layers. This enhances efficiency and reduces the required doses. ADAMA group has manufacturing facilities worldwide with key facilities in Neot Hovav, Beer Sheba, Ashdod, and Brazil. In addition, the group has smaller plants in Colombia, Poland, Spain, and Greece [4].

GFA (Grow Fish Anywhere) - Israel's GFA (Grow Fish Anywhere) Advanced Systems eliminates the environmental problems in conventional fish farming.

Specially developed microbes purify fish waste byproducts right in the tank, with no need for spillage and refilling. This system allows for high-capacity aquaculture, with as much as 100 kg of fish per cubic meter of water [4].

Hardier seeds- Hebrew University agricultural scientists Ilan Sela and Haim D. Rabinowitch developed TraitUP, a trademarked technology that enables the introduction of genetic materials into seeds without modifying their DNA. This method immediately and efficiently improves plants before they're even sowed [4].

List of Agriculture Companies

(Other Source of facts: http://nocamels.com/ and Wikipedia)

Solar Energy- Israel is building world's largest power station 'Ashalim' to produce 121 megawatts of renewable power to the country. The station will provide solar thermal energy, photovoltaic energy, and natural gas. A 30MW PV plant and a 121 MW CSP plant will be established by Megalim Solar Power, a joint venture between Brightsource and Alstom. The station is expected to commence electricity production in 2017. In the year 1950, Levi Yissar developed a revolutionary solar water heater to address the energy shortages of the country. In 1953, he started NerYah Company, Israel's first commercial manufacturer of solar water heaters and by 1967 around 50,000 solar heaters had been sold. With the 1970s oil crisis, Harry Zvi Tabor, father of Israeli solar energy, developed the solar water heater that now over 90% of Israeli homes use. The expertise of Israeli engineer and Israeli solar companies is needed worldwide. However, even though Israeli engineers have been involved in both photovoltaic and concentrated solar power, the Israeli companies which have become market leaders in their respective fields have all been involved in concentrated solar power.

Companies like BrightSource, Solel, and Brenmiller Energy deal with utility scale projects. Israel's goal is to produce ten percent of the country's energy from renewable sources by 2020. The electricity generated at the facility will be enough to supply 120,000 homes with clean energy and will avoid 110,000 tons of CO2 emissions each year over the course of its life. The Ministry of National Infrastructures estimates solar water heating saves Israel 2 million barrels of oil a year.

Solar Power Research:

The **Grand Technion Energy Program (GTEP)** started with an aim to bring together Technion's researchers to discover alternative and renewable energy sources, promote more efficient energy use, and reduce the environmental damage caused by the production of fossil fuels. GTEP is interdisciplinary, with members spanning the range from nanoscience to applied engineering.

Ben-Gurion National Solar Energy Center founded in 1987 by the Ministry of National Infrastructures to study alternative and clean energy technologies. In 2007, David Faiman, the director of the center, announced that the Center had entered into a project with Zenith Solar to create a home solar energy system that uses a 10-square meter reflector dish.

Jacob Blaustein Institutes for Desert Research- The Jacob Blaustein Institutes for Desert Research facility was founded by Amos Richmond in 1974. This institute conducts research in diverse fields and its solar energy research program has developed several innovative techniques that help in the development of passive heating, involving the mitigation of extremes of heat and cold in the desert through efficient storage from day to nighttime. A blend of 90 scientists, 60 technical and administrative staff members, and over 150 Israeli and foreign research students perform basic and applied research related to "Desert Sciences".

Weizmann Institute Solar Research Facilities Unit- The solar research facilities of the Weizmann Institute of Science are among the most advanced laboratories in the world for concentrated solar energy research. Tareq Abu-Hamed, an Israeli scientist at the University of Minnesota, with colleagues Jacob Karni and Michael Epstein, head of the Solar Facility at Weizmann, were the developers of a new method to produce hydrogen fuel more cheaply, efficiently and safely while solving storage and transportation issues. Other innovations include harnessing sunlight for space communications and meteorological information; controlling light-dependent chemical reactions; and developing photodynamic cancer therapy.

(Source of facts: Wikipedia, in.bgu.ac.il, and other government's website)

Military Engineering- As per the report 'Global Aerospace and Defense Outlook 2016' (published by Deloitte), Israel is 7th in the world in Defense spending. According to Globes, Israel spent $15.9 billion on its military overall in 2014.

Israel Defense Force (IDF) is famous for its modern technology, innovation in cyber warfare, intelligence, precision armaments and electronics. The IDF is one of the most technologically advanced armies in the world.

Sharing some of the most critical military capabilities of Israel [5]:

The IDF Unmanned Ground Vehicle- Guardium Unmanned Ground Vehicle (UGV) patrols the Israeli border without an onboard human presence. The Guardium is equipped with 360-degree cameras and a loudspeaker. It is highly mobile, which means that it can stream images from various angles and gather more data than a stationary camera can. Infantry soldiers often patrol alongside the Guardium, which can detect threats from a distance. If it spots something suspicious, the soldiers in the command room immediately notify the foot soldiers in the field of the danger.

Mobile Radar- IDF has developed a new mobile radar that will be attached to armored and infantry brigades, and will be able to respond immediately to rocket fire. The mobile radar will identify the source of fire against the brigade, including short-range shooting.

The Trophy System- Trophy is a military active protection system for vehicles. The trophy is the product of a ten-year collaborative development project between the Rafael Advanced Defense Systems and Israel Aircraft Industries' Elta Group. The main purpose is to supplement the armor of light and heavy armored fighting vehicles. The Trophy's detection system creates a 360-degree protective shield around the tank. This system instantly detects and neutralizes any threat to the tank by firing a missile of its own.

The Iron Dome Rocket Defense System-Iron Dome is a mobile all-weather air defense system developed by Rafael Advanced Defense Systems and Israel Aircraft Industries. The System has been deployed in the south of Israel since early 2011 in order to protect the citizens. On 10 March 2012, The Jerusalem Post reported that the system shot down 90% of rockets launched from Gaza that would have landed in populated areas. By November 2012, official statements indicated that it had intercepted 400+ rockets. By late October 2014, the Iron Dome systems had intercepted over 1,200 rockets. The system is the first of its kind in terms of speed, accuracy, and capability. As soon as an enemy rocket is fired into Israel, the radar station detects and tracks its trajectory and launches a missile of its own to intercept and neutralize the enemy rocket before it can cause any harm.

IDF's Dolphin-class Submarines - Israel's most critical military capability is their small but very deadly submarine fleet. The new submarine 'INS Rahav' is Israel's fifth Dolphin-class submarine. The new submarine is equipped with the most up-to-date naval weapons systems and improved detection capabilities. The INS Rehav is 220 feet long, it is capable of reaching a top speed of 25 knots underwater and can operate without resupply for up to 30 days under normal operating conditions. This new submarine uses air-independent propulsion (AIP) to stay submerged for weeks at a time and it is extremely quiet in comparison to its predecessors. Other boats in Israel's fleet are Dolphin, Tekuma, Leviathan and Tanin, the first three of which are Dolphin 1 class, with the Tanin being the first of the improved Dolphin 2 class. Dolphin class, in general, is based on Germany's highly successful line of submarines starting with the Type 209, but is most similar to the Type 212, although the Dolphin class is larger. The Dolphin 2 class is even larger than the Dolphin 1 class [6].

Israeli Military's Innovative products [7]:

PillCam- Given Imaging is an Israeli medical technology company. Given Imaging pioneered the capsule endoscopy technology with 'PillCam' a capsule with two tiny video cameras that enables visualization of patients' intestines without the need for endoscopy. This idea was developed by Dr. Gabi Iddan while working with missile division of Rafael, where he envisioned that missile technology could be miniaturized to create a medical product. He used miniature missile-guiding technology to craft this groundbreaking medical imaging device.

Emergency Bandage (Israeli Bandage) – It's a specifically designed first aid device that is used to stop bleeding from hemorrhagic wounds caused by traumatic injuries in pre-hospital emergency situations. It was invented by an Israeli military medic, Bernard Bar-Natan. Developed through Israel's Technology Incubator

Program, the Emergency Bandage saved so many US lives in Operation Iraqi Freedom and Operation Enduring Freedom that it became known as the Israeli Bandage in the North American market.

DiskOnKey USB flash drive—USB flash drives were invented by Amir Ban, Dov Moran, and Oron Ogdan. In 1989, Dov Moran founded the M-Systems and patented the first flash drive. They also created the True Flash Filing System (TrueFFS) which presented the flash memory as a disk drive to the computer. Dov Moran served Israeli navy for seven years and was commander of its microprocessors department. His M-Systems Flash Disk Pioneers Company was acquired by SanDisk in 2006.

Selman Surgical Rehearsal Platform- Retired Israel Air Force officers Moty Avisar and Alon Geri created a revolutionary neurosurgery simulator that lets brain surgeons rehearse challenging microsurgical procedures before making a single incision. The system generates 3D images from the patient's CT and MRI scans and provides a preview of how surgical instruments will interact with the patient's tissue and how the delicate brain structures will respond. It was launched at the Congress of Neurological Surgeons in October 2012 and is named after Dr. Warren Selman, the surgeon who commissioned the former officers to devise the system.

Through-Wall Vision- The Xaver (a product of Camero) through-wall radar imaging systems use 3D image reconstruction algorithms, signal processing techniques, and a unique proprietary sensor to generate 3D images of objects concealed behind cement, plaster, bricks, concrete or wood. The product line ranges from security cameras with advanced micropower radar technology to a handheld device intended for search-and-rescue workers. Amir Beeri (former head of IDF's R&D department) after spending 14-plus years in military intelligence, in 2004 founded Camero. Now Camero is a leader in development and marketing of radar-based imaging systems. Camero is a part of the SK GROUP, a leading global defense and security group that includes Israel Weapons Industries(IWI), Meprolight, Israel Shipyards, PI Systems, Uniscope and more.

IAI Heron- The IAI Heron is a medium-altitude long endurance unmanned aerial vehicle (UAV) developed by the Malat (UAV) division of Israel Aerospace Industries. It is capable of Medium Altitude Long Endurance (MALE) operations of up to 52 hours duration at up to 10.5 km (35,000 ft). Heron can carry an array of sensors, including thermographic camera (infrared) and visible-light airborne ground surveillance, intelligence systems (COMINT and ELINT) and various radar systems, totaling up to 250 kg (550 lb). Heron is also capable of target acquisition and artillery adjustment.

IDF has developed several other critical and innovative military products, these are the most talked about, Israel is truly a leader in military engineering.

(There are many other interesting products, you can read in detail at http://www.israel21c.org/20-top-technology-inventions-born-of-conflict/)

Hi-Tech Companies-

Israel is a hub of thousands of high technology companies in a wide range of fields such as telecommunications equipment, software, semiconductors, biotechnology and medical electronics. High-tech companies are located throughout the country: in central Tel Aviv, in the suburbs of Jerusalem, even in development towns in the Galilee and the Negev. But the main centers are in Tel Aviv's Atidim Industrial Park, to the north of Tel Aviv in Herzliya Pituah, and to the south in Rehovot, adjacent to the Weizmann Institute, as well as in Tel Aviv's northeastern suburbs [8].

There are over 250 MNCs research and development centers in Israel, 80 of them Fortune 500 companies including a large number of US companies. The world's most important tech companies run Israeli research centers, including Cisco, Microsoft, Google, Apple, IBM, Oracle, SAP, EMC, Motorola, HP, Facebook, and eBay.

Let's take a look at some major R&D centers and their contributions [9]:

Intel: Intel is an American MNC and one of the largest and highest valued semiconductor chip maker based on revenue. It is the inventor of the x86 and x64 series of microprocessors, the processors found in most personal computers. In March 2014, Intel embarked a $6billion plan to expand its activities in Israel.

Notable contributions of Intel's Israeli R&D Center: the development of the first PC processor, the 8088 (used by IBM for its machines) in 1979 by Intel's Haifa team, the Pentium MMX processor released in 1997 the most widely distributed processor of the 20th century also developed in Haifa, development of the various generations of the Pentium laptop processors (Dothan, Banias, etc.) as well as the Centrino processor, the first laptop processor with Wi-Fi, development and production of the latest Intel tech, including Thunderbolt, Sandy Bridge, Ivy Bridge etc.

Google: Google's Israeli R&D center has done significant work in search, innovations like Google Suggest, Google In-Page Analytics, and YouTube Annotations. Google Israel's work in digitizing text 'The Digital Dead Sea Scrolls' project allow users to examine and explore these most ancient manuscripts from Second Temple times. Google and Israel Museum partnered for this project. The website gives users access to searchable, fast-loading, high-resolution images of the scrolls, as well as short explanatory videos and background information on the texts and their history. The project, started by a single engineer in Google's Haifa office, has become the standard for more ambitious Google digitizing projects, with the Paris office using the system developed in Israel to digitize what will eventually be thousands of historic archives and documents.

HP: HP has eight major facilities in Israel, one dedicated to the country's local business along with seven R&D centers. Established in 1994, Hewlett-Packard Labs Israel is an excellence center focusing on research in big data analysis, machine learning, and data mining. The Haifa lab is taking the lead in reinventing analytics for the era of Memory-driven Computing and in building the platforms, technologies, and tools required to gather, synthesize and interpret massive volumes of data in real-time.

IBM- IBM Research - Haifa is the largest lab of IBM Research Division outside of the United States. Founded as a small scientific center in 1972, it grew into a major lab that leads the development of innovative technological products and solutions for the IBM corporation. The Lab works with IBM development and services arms, partners with clients to answer their needs, and collaborates with universities to promote industrial research. Its major projects are related to cloud, storage, big data, social analytics, mobile, security, and quality. The lab also focuses on two industry domains: healthcare and retail.

IBM Israel also has a software lab ILSL and cybersecurity center of excellence.

Marvell Technology Group- A producer of storage, communications and consumer semiconductor products. The company was founded in 1995 and has approximately 7,500 employees, 1,200 of whom, or nearly 20%, are in Israel.

Marvell Software Solutions Israel is a wholly owned subsidiary of Marvell Technology group that specializes in LAN technologies.

Directory of Israeli hi-tech companies: http://www.science.co.il/companies/

Silicon Wadi, a hub of high-tech industries in Israel, similar to Silicon Valley in California, US, it is one of the world's most dynamic startup ecosystems. The area covers much of the country, although especially high concentrations of hi-tech industry can be found in the area around Tel Aviv, including small clusters around the cities of Ra'anana, Petah Tikva, Herzliya, Netanya, the academic city of Rehovot and its neighbor Rishon Le Zion. In addition, hi-tech clusters can be found in Haifa and Caesarea. More recent hi-tech establishments have been raised in Jerusalem, and in towns such as Yokneam Illit and Israel's first "private city," Airport City, near Tel Aviv. (Source: Wikipedia)

Startup Nation-As per the recent rankings, Tel Aviv, Israel's capital city, ranks number five in the top 20 global startup ecosystems in the world. Israel's startup ecosystem is vibrant. Tel Aviv provides all the platforms that are necessary to facilitate innovation and R&D, simple administrative procedures create ease of doing business environment and foster entrepreneurship. Israel Prime Minister Benjamin Netanyahu has said "As far as the 'startup nation' I think this has a lot to do with **entrepreneurial spirit**. I have noticed that in Silicon Valley (USA), you hear Indian dialects and you hear Hebrew, sometimes you hear some English, which means there is a lot of spirit for enterprise in both our countries." Few days back Israeli-born billionaire Haim Saban has announced to set up a new fund to invest $100 million in Israeli startups. The fund will invest in startups in the mobile, social networks, e-commerce, and digital media sectors. Israeli startups are known for cutting-edge technologies, advanced medical devices, FinTech solutions, cyber security, IoT and cool gadgets and apps. Israel's spirit and innovation culture are remarkable. **Let's take a look at some popular and innovative Israeli Startups and their products** [10]:

Dojo Labs- Dojo labs designed a security technology that gets connects to the network and acts as the essential layer between smart devices and security/privacy threats. It monitors all data sent by anything connected to the Internet. If Dojo observes any suspicious activity it sends alert on Dojo mobile app and allow the user to remotely turn the device off or block its communications. Dojo is founded in 2014 by Yossi Atias and Smulik Bachar.

SniffPhone- Designed by Prof. Hossam Haick of Technion Institute, this device can sense disease on the breath. SniffPhone uses nanotechnology to analyze breath and it is able to detect lung cancer as well. SniffPhone is a mobile device that can be taken to anywhere, which makes it useful for rural areas.

ZUtA Labs- ZUtA is a mini robotic printer; it connects directly to smartphone and to PCs and allows the user to print on any size piece of paper. This printer is designed by Israeli firm Nekuda, it works on Bluetooth and wireless networks. ZUtA is founded in 2014 by Tuvia Elbaum and Matan Caspi, ZUtA (which means "small" in Hebrew) and it won the best of innovation award at CES 2015.

SkySaver- SkySaver is an emergency backpack that's designed to escape from high-rises when a fire breaks out. This lifesaving kit equipped with a cable cord of approximately 80 meters that, in the case of an emergency, is attached to a pre-installed anchor located near a window. When a fire breaks out, the emergency device is strapped on with buckles that wrap around the waist and between the legs. Founded in 2012 by Eli Gross, SkySaver is truly a life saver!

Singlecue- Singlecue designed by EyeSight Technologies is a home automation device. Through Singlecue, you can control your TV, media and smart homes devices using touch-free gestures. Just lift your finger and get control over the devices. This device can recognize almost anything with an infrared, Wi-Fi, or Bluetooth sensor. Launched in 2014, Singlecue is a cool gadget in IoT space.

Tridom- Urban development startup Tridom designed a 3D-printed space home for NASA. Founded in 2014 by Yaron Schwarcz and Lior Aharoni, Tridom presented in September a model of an inflatable structure that could be blown up with a small amount of liquefied natural gas once on Planet Mars.

Pixie- Pixie's technology uses a Location-of-Things platform to derive the precise location of our valuables at all times. The system uses Pixie Points, the smart tags that we can affix to anything (even your pet) and a mobile app. After attaching this tag the object gets pixified that is it joins a closed, private network of all of the pixified items that smartphone keeps track of via Bluetooth. Pixie app displays an augmented reality view using your smartphone's camera. Each Pixie Point has a 50-foot range indoors and a 150-foot range outdoors. Pixie is founded in 2011 by Amir Bassan-Eskenazi and Ofer Friedman.

G-RO- It's a smart suitcase that charges our phone and laptop on the go. G-RO is developed by Israeli startup Travel-Light, founded by Netta Shalgi and Ken Hertz, the product was launched in October 2015.

HomeBioGas- This biodigester turns organic waste into fertilizers and biofuel for cooking. It's a new "Off the Grid" biogas system, produces daily clean cooking gas for 3 meals and 10 liters of clean natural liquid fertilizer. It is really an amazing product for home and environment. HomeBioGas is founded by Ron Gonen and Thomas H. Cullhane.

Cyber Security- The combination of Israel's defense expertise and technological capabilities has turned Cyber security into one of its most important exports. According to Israel's National Cyber Bureau, Israel accounted for 10 percent of global security technology and sales of its security software topped $60 billion in 2014.

In the words of Dudu Mimran, CTO of the Cyber Security Research Center at Ben-Gurion University "The challenging environment Israel faces in the Middle East in the physical world has reflections also on the cyber world. Security is a subject that can be taught theoretically, but nothing is a substitute for a real hands-on experience and we've got lots of it." Israel's cyber security ecosystem is a perfect blend of mature companies like Check Point, venture capitalists such as Jerusalem Venture Partners (JVP) Cyber Labs and research collaborations such as the Deutsche Telekom Innovation Laboratories and Ben-Gurion University [11]. Some popular Israeli cyber security companies are:

CyberArk Software, Imperva Data Center Security Solutions, ThetaRay, CyberSeal, BioCatch, Seculert, Votiro, Argus Cyber Security, SenseCy, Check Point Software Technologies, Covertix, and Lacoon Mobile Security.

Advanced Technology Park of Israel: In Sep' 2013 Israel's Prime Minister Benjamin Netanyahu inaugurated Advanced Technology Park on the campus of Ben Gurion University in Be'er Sheva. The primary mission of the Advanced Technologies Park is to promote technology and commercialization of cutting-edge research and innovation being developed through BGU (BEN-GURION UNIVERSITY) and affiliate institutions. ATP creates a symbiotic relationship between three potent entities: Academe, Tech companies, and Israeli Defense Force. Dr. Moti Herskowitz (Dean of Research and Development, BGU) said "Our research model is that we have no model, which is the strength of it. We deal with it case by case". I appreciate his view because R&D team should think like this. One of the BGU's key catalysts in bridging the gap between academe and industry is its commercialization arm, BGN Technologies, which uses a unique model of technology transfer, under this model the university takes valuable ideas and brings them to market by partnering with a company or selling the company a patent. So far BGN Technologies has signed agreements with over 150 companies, including ExxonMobile, Johnson & Johnson, Siemens, and General Motors. BGN Technologies has been so successful at this that universities from the U.S. and Europe are studying their approach [12].

In this case study, I have covered the most attractive sectors of Israel and I believe there is still a lot to cover. While I was writing this case study, I observed the latest trends of BDS movement. Boycott, Divestment, and Sanctions is a campaign that was started in July 2005 by Palestinian NGOs to make economic and social pressure on Israel. I believe Israel, as a nation is accustomed to handling all this and such trends can not affect the spirit of Israel.

Singapore – Case Study

Singapore is a vibrant nation; it has attained a leading global position in telecommunication, financial services, professional services and transport infrastructure. According to the World Bank Doing Business 2016 report, Singapore is the easiest country to do business. Singapore's strategic position makes it attractive to global investors. In the month of January 2016, Singapore Prime Minister Lee Hsien Loong announced the plan for Research, Innovation and Enterprise (RIE) 2020. Under this initiative, Singapore government has allocated $19 billion towards developing Singapore as a knowledge-based and innovation-driven economy. Mr. Lee Hsien Loong always put emphasis on technology and the entrepreneurial spirit. On the occasion of Smart Nation Launch he said "we need the skills, we need the education, and the "can-do" spirit of experimenting and risk-taking. This is what makes Silicon Valley special, the world leader in technology innovation, a constant churn of ideas, of new business models."

Singapore is the fourth leading financial center in the world (GFCI - Global Financial Centers Index 2015). Singapore economy is characterized by the corruption-free environment, skilled workforce, low tax rates and advanced infrastructure. Singapore government uses a proactive strategy to attract FDI, as per the 'UNCTAD 2015 World Investment Report', Singapore is the 5th largest recipient of FDI in the world and the 3rd largest in the East and Southeast Asian countries. There are more than 7,000 foreign MNCs and around 10,000 foreign SMEs from around the world which have set up base in Singapore. It continues to be well-regarded as a triple-A rated economy.

(Source of facts: Wikipedia and financial reports)

Singapore has emerged as an innovation hub at the cutting-edge of modern business. During last few years a huge entrepreneurial ecosystem is being developed in Singapore. According to Compass's 'Global Startup Ecosystem Ranking 2015' Singapore is the 10th best startup ecosystem in the world.

One of the top contributors to Singaporean economy is "Financial Services"; let's take a look at some interesting aspects:

Singapore- A Leading Financial Hub:

Singapore's financial sector is astonishing, over 200 banks have a presence in Singapore and a growing number have chosen to base their operational headquarters here to service their regional group activities. With a total asset size of almost US$2 trillion as of December 2013, the banking sector has been critical to Singapore's role in financing local and regional growth, for example, in facilitating trade, corporate finance and the building of infrastructure. Singapore has a dominant presence in other countries through its financial giants such as DBS Group, United Overseas Bank, and OCBC Bank. Singapore's physical infrastructure, logistical capabilities, political and economic stability gives traders the confidence to invest in Singapore.

Capital Markets

Markets for trading debt and equity instruments are Capital Markets. Capital markets are concentrated in financial centers such New York, London, Singapore and Hong Kong. A key element of Singapore's financial center is its deep and liquid capital markets.

Debt Capital Markets: Singapore's bond market has grown in depth and breadth over the past decade. There are enormous opportunities exist for fixed income investors because a range of both Singapore government securities and foreign corporate bonds are available. Bond offerings with a lower minimum subscription size and tradable on the Singapore Exchange (SGX) are also available for the retail market.

Equity Capital Markets: Singapore Exchange (SGX) is the preferred listing location for close to 800 companies. SGX is a member of World Federation of Exchange and the Asian and Oceanian Stock Exchanges Federation. About 40% of SGX's listings are foreign companies, across regions such as Asia-Pacific, particularly in South East Asia, and further afield in Europe and America. There are strong listings in diverse sectors such as real estate, shipping and offshore marine and infrastructure. Singapore is a growing market for REIT (Real Estate Investment Trust) in Asia Pacific.

Foreign Exchange

Foreign exchange (FX) and OTC derivatives market are crucial to the success of Singapore's financial and international market. There are major global FX dealers that offer a deep and liquid market for trading and hedging of G3 currencies (US dollar, euro, and Japanese yen), as well as Asian emerging market currencies. According to the latest 2013 Triennial survey by the Bank for International Settlements (BIS), the average daily FX turnover volume in Singapore was US$383 billion in April 2013. This survey ranked Singapore as the third-largest FX center in the world and the largest FX center in Asia Pacific. Singapore was also ranked the largest OTC interest rate derivatives center in Asia Pacific excluding Japan by turnover. This reflects Singapore's position as an international financial center and a major treasury center in the region. (Source of facts: mas.gov.sg)

Singapore-based DBS has topped the Southeast Asian banks in Global Finance magazine's World's Best Foreign Exchange Banks and Providers survey. DBS is an active FX market maker, with an extensive branch network across Asia and a leading market share in Southeast Asia. It has the biggest FX team among local banks in its home market, as well as FX operations in Hong Kong, China, India, Indonesia, Taiwan, South Korea and Vietnam [13].

Wealth Management and Insurance

Asset Management: According to Singapore Asset Management Survey (conducted by Monetary Authority of Singapore) Singapore's assets under management ("AUM") rose to S$2.4 trillion in 2014 [14]. Singapore is considered as one of the leading asset management centers in Asia. Diverse communities of asset managers exist in Singapore, this involves globally recognized traditional players and alternative players, including the hedge fund, private equity, and real estate managers.

Private Banking- Singapore is an attractive center for private banking due to its strong legal system, security and efficient wealth services. Singapore is Asia's second-largest offshore center by assets; it manages US$470 billion of private client assets [15]. On 5th April 2011, PBAG (private banking advisory group) has launched a Private Banking Code of Conduct for the industry. The Code of conduct aimed at improving the competency of private banking professionals and establishing high market conduct standards. To read more in detail about PB Code, you can visit the website of the Association of Banks in Singapore (ABS) at www.abs.org.sg.

According to annual rankings (2015) by Private Banker International, a journal for the global wealth industry, Singapore's DBS bank is an 8th largest private bank in Asia-Pacific. In the top 20 private banks of Asia Pacific ranking, other Singaporean banks like OCBC and UOB positioned at number 11 and 17 respectively [16]. These numbers show the strength of Private Banking in Singapore.

Insurance- According to the report of a global reinsurance giant Swiss Re, in the coming years Asia's insurance market is expected to see annual growth of 12% in non-life insurance and 13% in life insurance. By 2020, Asia is likely to account for almost 40% of the global market. Singapore's current Prime Minister Lee Hsein Loong's one of the vision areas is to establish Singapore as a global insurance hub by 2020.

Today, Singapore is a center of direct insurers, reinsurers, and captive insurers. A large number of major international insurers and reinsurers are based in Singapore. Local and international players offer a range of insurance services to meet the needs of the domestic market. Several reinsurers and captive insurers also use Singapore as a base to write risks from the region. A good network of insurance intermediaries and supplementary service providers has also emerged. World's leading insurance broking, captive management, and risk management brands operate in Singapore.

RBC2- Revision to Risk Based Capital Framework- Last year The Monetary Authority of Singapore has revised the risk-based capital framework. To read in detail about the revision in Risk-based capital framework and its impact, you can read this report:

http://www.kpmg.com/sg/en/issuesandinsights/articlespublications/documents/advisory-insurance-revisions-to-the-risk-based-capital-framework.pdf

Singapore Innovative Startup Ecosystem- During last few years Singapore has emerged as a major hub for technology startups in Southeast Asia. Transparent and corruption free government systems, supportive business and financial structures make Singapore a perfect choice for aspiring entrepreneurs. According to Compass's 'Startup Ecosystem Ranking 2015' report, Singapore is the 10th best startup ecosystem in the world.

Some innovative and popular gadgets designed in Singapore are [17]:

Touch Plus: Designed by Darren Lim, a smart young Singaporean Touch Plus is an ambitious motion capturing device. It tracks hand gestures and allows to control iOS and Android devices, tablets, and smart TVs by tapping or swiping on any surface.

InkCase Plus: InkCase Plus is the 2nd generation InkCase with enhanced features and performance. InkCase displays any picture you want on the back of the phone, including weather forecasts, your daily To Do List. InkCase's E-Paper technology and low power consumption complete your eBook reading experience on a Smartphone without hurting your eyes or worrying about draining the phone's battery.

TouchPico: A slim projector that transforms any flat surface into an 80-inch touchscreen. It's like an android tablet with projected touch interface and wireless streaming that allows to project an 80-inch display to any flat surface and also to interact with it using infrared stylus.

Zensorium: A compact device that measures heart rate, variability, blood oxygen level and respiratory rate. To use it, simply plug it into your smartphone, put your finger on the sensor, and the device will deliver readings to you in seconds. It's a good product for wellness and health sensitive people.

CreoPop: Creo Pop is a venture backed, Singapore-based company, founded by Andreas Birnik and Dmitry Starodubtsev. Cero Pop is a 3D printing pen that lets you draw shapes into the air through solidifying ink using UV light. In contrast, to other 3D pens, CreoPop uses photopolymers that are solidified using LED diodes to let users create amazing 3D designs. CreoPop also offers the large selection of cool inks including different colors, elastic ink, magnetic ink, glow-in-the-dark ink, temperature sensitive ink and body paint ink.

Rotimatic: It's a robotic roti maker, a product of Zimplistic, it makes healthy homemade rotis automatically, the user need to just fill the ingredients into it and press a button to give input about roti specification and it will produce plenty of rotis. Zimplistic is founded by Pranoti Nagarkar and Rishi Israni.

Top 10 Singapore Startups:

Garena- Garena was founded in Singapore by Forrest Li and his friends, it's a consumer internet platform provider with 17 million active monthly users on the PC and 11 million on mobile. In 2010, Garena launched its first product Garena+, an online game, and social platform to search, download and play online games. Garena is a leading platform provider for online entertainment and communication tools across Southeast Asia, Taiwan, and Hong Kong. Garena has partnerships with game developers including Riot Games and Electronic Arts. (Source: Wikipedia)

Lazada- Lazada group was founded by Rocket Internet in 2011, with a goal to establish 'Amazon.com of Southeast Asia'. Rocket Internet is a German incubator that builds companies that copy the business models of successful US tech companies. As of 2014, Lazada Group operated sites in Indonesia, Malaysia, the Philippines, Singapore, Thailand, and Vietnam. (Source: Wikipedia)

RedMart- The Company was founded in November 2011 by Roger Egan, Vikram Rupani, and Rajesh Lingappa. RedMart is Singapore's online supermarket.

iCarsclub- iCarsClub is Asia's online peer to peer car sharing platform. It allows car owners to list their cars to earn money during their car's idle time and car drivers to rent a car at a relatively lower rate. (Website: http://www.icarsclub.com/)

MatchMove pay-MatchMove Pay is Singapore's finance technology company, that provide innovative enterprise solutions. It is founded in 2009 by Shailesh Naik. In 2014, MatchMove Pay launched the MatchMove Wallet, a mobile payment card, in partnership with American Express. The MatchMove Wallet is a Platform-as-a-Service (PaaS) that enables any major consumer brands, banks, telcos and regional e-commerce sites to easily issue secure mobile payment cards to reach potential shoppers with smartphones in Asia and emerging markets. The wallet also supports other major networks like MasterCard, Visa, Union Pay and JCB. The company was also ranked as Singapore's fastest-growing technology company in Southeast Asia in the Deloitte Technology Fast 500 Asia Pacific in 2013 and also awarded the Red Herring Top 100 Asia and Red Herring 100 Global in 2012. (Source: http://matchmovepay.com/)

Viki- Razmig Hovaghimian, Changseong Ho, and Jiwon Moon founded Viki in 2007. Viki is a video streaming website based in Singapore that offers on-demand streaming video of TV shows, movies, and music videos from around the world. The company has offices in Singapore, San Francisco, Indonesia, and Seoul, South Korea. In 2013, Japanese Firm Rakuten has acquired Viki in $200 million. In the year following its acquisition by Rakuten, Viki went from about 22 million monthly active users with 10 million on mobile to 35 million monthly active users and 25 million mobile users. (Source: Wikipedia)

MyRepublic- MyRepublic was founded in 2011 by Malcolm Rodrigues, KC Lai, and Greg Mittman. MyRepublic is fourth-largest internet service provider in Singapore. It offers services in New Zealand and Indonesia too. As of 2015, MyRepublic offers internet speeds of 200 Mbit/s – 1 Gbit/s to residential customers and 100 Mbit/s – 1 Gbit/s to the corporate customer in Singapore.

(Source: Wikipedia)

DocDoc- DocDoc is founded in 2012, by veteran professionals from both the Healthcare and Technology industries. It is an online medical appointment reservation and healthcare information portal. More than 500,000 engaged users search for health-related information and healthcare services each month, making DocDoc the largest pan-Asian digital healthcare portal.

(Source: www.docdoc.sg)

FastaCash- Founded in 2012, fastacash is a leading FinTech startup of Singapore, which provides a social payments platform to transfer value (money, airtime, other tokens of value etc.) along with digital content (photos, videos, audio, messages etc.) through social networks and messaging platforms. FastCash has received good coverage in Asia's leading business media. (Source: www.fastacash.com)

Anacle Systems- Anacle Systems is a technology company. Founded in 2006, Anacle System offers innovative solutions for a wide range of industry sectors like Facility Management, Aerospace, Healthcare, Manufacturing, Utilities, Oil & Gas,

Telecommunications, Education, Retail Mall and Government. In 2015, Anacle System won Frost and Sullivan Singapore Energy Management Company of the Year Award. (Source: www.anacle.com)

There are dozens of interesting startups in Singapore, many of them clustered in Block 71, it is located in Singapore's Ayer Rajah Industrial Estate, a building close to INSEAD, the National University of Singapore, and government-sponsored innovation and research centers Fusionopolis and Biopolis.

Block 71- The Economist referred to 'Blk71' as the heart of Singapore's technology start-up ecosystem and the world's most tightly packed entrepreneurial ecosystem. In 2011, NUS Enterprise, the Media Development Authority, and SingTel Innov8 collaborated to set up an incubation program 'Plug-In@Blk71', the goal was to bring the interactive digital media/ info-communications start-up cluster, which was previously dispersed around Singapore, under one roof. Soon after this initiative, Blk71 turned into a flourishing start-up hub. Block 71 is a successful experiment of Singapore Government, it has set an example of administrative innovation and now hundreds of tech startups, venture funds, and incubators are operating and collaborating at Blk71. Inspired by the success of Blk71, the cluster is expanded further with JTC LauncPad @onenorth, a joint initiative of A*STAR, iDA, MDA, NRF and SPRING, it comprises three blocks - the current Blk 71 Ayer Rajah Crescent and two new blocks – Blk 73 and Blk 79. This expansion is a significant move for Singapore startups community.

(Source: Wikipedia and Government's official websites)

The founding father of Singapore is Mr. Lee Kuan Yew (LKY), under his leadership Singapore transitioned from "the third world to the first world ", he said ('Wit and Wisdom' book) "I do not yet know of a man who became a leader as a result of having undergone a leadership course." I believe when the leadership of the country inspires people to innovate nothing else can stop them. Singapore's leaders have played their part perfectly and its results are quite visible.

India- An Emerging Innovation Economy

The Indian government has adopted a Lean Management approach in each sector and sub-sector of the economy be it Agriculture, Industry, Services, Railway, Manufacturing, Administration, Jurisdiction, and Law. Prime Minister Mr. Narendra Modi says that "Innovation is the need of the hour, for every society and every era", he is doing everything possible to make enterprise and innovation easier. During early days of his government Mr. Modi has announced that his government will identify and eliminate all those policies and procedures that are creating waste in the system, since then the government is working to simplify all those policies that are needed for economic growth like Startup policies, Tax policies, FDI policies, Foreign Trade policy, employment rules and labour policies and oil and gas exploration regulations. Notable steps taken so far in this direction are: Goods and Services Tax (GST) that aims to simplify the complex Indian tax system, converting 44 labor laws into four simplified codes, Introduction of composite caps for simplification of Foreign Direct Investment (FDI) policy and Startup Action Plan- a simple form to register startup from mobile or desktop, fast tracking of patent applications, faster exit for startup etc.

At the time of global economic turbulence, India is emerging as a new hope for the world economy. India now ranks 130 out of 189 countries in the ease of doing business. India's economy became the world's fastest-growing major economy from the last quarter of 2014. India also topped the World Bank's growth outlook for 2015-16 for the first time with the economy having grown 7.6% in 2015-16 and expected to grow 7.7-8.0% in 2016-17. According to the IMF, the Indian economy is the "bright spot" in the global landscape. India's retail market worth was $600 billion in 2015 and it is one of the world's fastest growing E-Commerce markets.
(Source of the facts: Wikipedia)

Prime Minister Mr. Narendra Modi has infused all Indian with a sense of pride; he inspires people to innovate through his pro-business approach and moves. To establish India as a world leader in Innovation Economy, Prime Minister has taken three major initiatives- Make in India, Digital India, and Startup India. India is witnessing a new era of innovation and opportunities. To introduce innovation in existing processes, it is necessary to simplify or eliminate those processes that creating hurdles in smooth functioning and not adding any value to the system.

Let's take a look at some major initiatives taken by the government to foster a culture of innovation and entrepreneurship and how Indian government is applying lean management principle in administration.

Agriculture- The agricultural sector is the largest employer in India's economy, India ranks second worldwide in farm output. Agriculture and allied sectors like forestry, logging and fishing accounted for 17% of the GDP and employed 49% of the total workforce in 2014. Indian Government is trying to improve agriculture sector through the fusion of traditional farming practices and modern technology. Government is setting up a National Agricultural Marketing Platform; it's a virtual for farmers. Under this 550 mandis would be integrated with its network. Through 'Pradhan Mantri Mudra Yojana' government is encouraging youth to launch Startups in the farm sector too. Let's take a look at some notable innovative initiatives:

Rurban Mission- National Rurban Mission is based on the idea of a smart village. It aims to encourage social, economic and infrastructure development in rural areas by developing a cluster of 300 smart villages over next 3 years across the country. It's a unique idea of combining urban and rural India, PM referred to Rurbans as territories 'with the soul of village and facilities of city'. Main components of Rurban Mission are: Skill development training, Agro Processing/Agro Storage Services and Warehousing, Sanitation, Digital Literacy, Solid and liquid waste management, Provision of piped water supply, Village streets and drains, Street lights, Upgrading school/higher education facilities, fully equipped mobile health unit, Service Centers for electronic delivery of citizen centric services/e-gram connectivity, Public transport, Inter-village road connectivity and LPG gas connections [18].

Innovative Crop Insurance Scheme- The central theme of this innovative crop insurance scheme is 'Minimum Premium, Maximum Insurance' for farmers. Main features of this scheme are: For the first time emphasis has been given to mobile and satellite technology to facilitate accurate assessment, farmers will pay the lowest ever premium rate, only one premium rate for each season, removing all variations in rates across crops and districts within a season, the flood is included under localized risk cover, post-harvest losses arising out of cyclones and unseasonal rain have been covered. (Source: prime minister's official website)

Innovations in Agriculture- Indian Startups [19]-

CropIn Technology Solutions- Founded by Bangalore based software engineers, Krishna Kumar and Kunal Prasad. CropIn Technology is using technology, mobile, and big data to improve crop traceability and sustainability. CropIn offers cloud and mobile based analytical solutions through an android based mobile app 'Smart Farms'.

Main features of this app:

--It helps to raise pest/disease alert with images and voice recording from farms in few seconds and shared with an expert for real-time advice.

--Maintain history of all pest and diseases along with advice was given by expert and their analysis.

--Send Bulk SMS to reach out farmers and farm field force for a specific action plan.

--Schedule package of practices notification and broadcast to farmers based on the date of sowing/plantation.

Website: http://cropin.co.in/

Eruvaka Technologies- Founded by Sreeram Raavi and Mark Kahn, Eruvaka Technologies works in aquaculture sector, it offers on-farm diagnostic equipment for aquaculture farmers to reduce their risk and increase productivity. Eruvaka provides tools that are integrated with sensors and mobile connectivity for aquaculture monitoring and automation. Website: www.eruvaka.com

Skymet- It's a weather monitoring and agri-risk solutions company. Skymet has developed technologies and instruments to measure weather and agriculture for different range of users like small and marginal farmers, urban dwellers, energy companies (renewable and non-renewable), insurance companies, governments and international NGOs. Skymet is -backed by Omnivore Partners & DMGI.

Website: http://www.skymet.net/

Ekgaon- The company is headquarters in New Delhi with its regional office in Madurai (Tamil Nadu) and Mandla (Madhya Pradesh) in India. It's key markets are India, South Asia, and Africa. Ekgaon offers a mobile phone enabled financial services delivery platform and 'OneVillageOneWorld' Network platform that offers a range of services to farmers in rural areas including financial, agricultural inputs and government assistance. Website: https://ekgaon.com

FrontalRain Technologies- Bangalore based FrontalRain Technologies offers Social, Mobile, Analytics and Cloud Computing Software for Food and Agribusinesses. Its product Rain+ helps agribusinesses and emerging companies to use technology to manage every stage of crop growth right from planning, preparation, growing and harvesting to the clearing.

Website: http://www.frontalrain.com/

Agrostar- It's a Pune based, M-Commerce platform that enables farmers to procure a range of agricultural goods such as seeds, crop nutrition, crop protection and agri-hardware products by simply giving a missed call on the company's toll free number or through their mobile app. Agrostar currently operates in the states of Gujarat, Maharashtra, Madhya Pradesh and Rajasthan. Farmers in these states can procure an entire range of good quality and branded agri-inputs.

Website: http://www.agrostar.in/

Barrix- Started in 2011, Bangalore-based Barrix Pvt. Ltd offers eco-friendly crop protection methods and performs Research Activities in agriculture sciences.

Its Main Products are Barrix Catch Fruit/Veg Fly Trap and Fly Lure, Fly pest sticky sheet (yellow sheet and blue sheet), Barrix chromatic trap yellow roll and different fruit and vegetable crops cultivators. Barrix Agro Sciences is a venture backed by Omnivore Partners - venture capitalists and CIIE – incubator.

Website: http://www.barrix.in/

Anulekh- Mumbai-based Anulekh focuses on increasing soil fertility to achieve higher agricultural productivity and crop yield with lower resource use. Anulekh has launched a product BIOSAT that reduces resource consumption and increases food production. Website: http://www.anulekh.com/

Mitra- Nasik-based startup, MITRA (Machines, Information, Technology, Resources for Agriculture) aims to improve mechanization at horticulture farms with the use of R&D and high-quality farm equipment. MITRA develops proprietary agricultural machines that automate labor-intensive functions for farmers. Website: http://mitraweb.in/

Kisan Raja-Vijay Bhaskar has developed Kisan Raja, a GSM based controller, which allows the farmer to control the agricultural motor using his mobile or landline. Kisan Raja is among the top-5 innovations at the Samsung Innovation Quotient Conducted by CNBC-TV 18 in 2011.

Website: http://www.kisanraja.com/

Make In India- "Come, make in India", "Come, manufacture in India". Sell in any country of the world but manufacture here. We have got skill, talent, discipline, and determination to do something. We want to give the world a favorable opportunity that come here, "Come, Make in India" and we will say to the world, from electrical to electronics, "Come, Make in India", from automobiles to agro value addition "Come, Make in India", paper or plastic, "Come, Make in India", satellite or submarine "Come, Make in India". Our country is powerful. Come, I am giving you an invitation", these are the words of Prime Minister Mr. Narendra Modi (first Independence Day Speech). The 'Make in India' program is launched to boost manufacturing in India. Through this initiative government is encouraging overseas companies to set up their units in India as well as encouraging domestic companies to increase production within the country. Through Make in India program government wants to increase the domestic value addition and technological depth in manufacturing. This aims to enhance the global competitiveness of the Indian manufacturing sector. Transparency and simple processes are the main factors in the success of Make in India, so far several steps have been taken by the government to improve the ease of doing business in India, the aim is to de-license and de-regulate the industry during the entire life cycle of a business. Let's a take look [20]: (Source: www.dnaindia.com)

-- Environment clearances can be sought online.

-- All income tax returns can be filed online.

-- Validity of industrial license is extended to three years.

-- Paper registers are replaced by electronic registers.

-- Approval of the head of the department is necessary to undertake an inspection.

Foreign Direct Investment (FDI):

100 % FDI is allowed in all sectors except Space (74%), Defense (49%) and News Media (26%). FDI restrictions in tea plantation have been removed while the FDI limit in defense sector has been raised from 26% to 49%.

The government has decided to improve and protect the intellectual property rights of innovators and creators by upgrading infrastructure, and using state-of-the-art technology. Patent filing procedures have been simplified and there is 80% rebate in the filing of the patent for startups.

The vision of India's leadership is to make India a global manufacturing hub. The government wants to increase manufacturing sector growth to 12-14% per annum so that the share of manufacturing in the country's Gross Domestic Product go up from16% to 25% by 2022. Through this program government wants to create 100 million additional jobs in manufacturing sector. A nationwide "skill India" movement is also initiated to improve employability. 'Make in India' has identified 25 sectors in manufacturing, infrastructure and service activities.

This initiative intends to change the Industry's mindset by changing the way Government interacts with industry. This new approach will be that of a facilitator and not that of a regulator.

Railway and Innovation- Indian railway has set an example of 'Innovation in Administration'. The railway is focusing on an innovative approach to find solutions to complex administrative problems.

SUTRA (Special Unit for Transportation Research and Analytics) – Railway Minister in this year's rail budget shared the ideas of SUTRA, a dedicated cross-functional team, that would comprise professional analysts, best in class decision support systems and optimization engines. Indian railway collects 100 terabytes of data each year, now this team will perform in-depth analysis on this data with the help of expert system to gain business insights and to optimize investment decisions and operations [21].

Kayakalp- This year Indian Railway has set up an innovation committee called 'Kayakalp', Mr. Ratan Tata will head this committee and it will comprise reputed investors, representatives from National Academy of Indian Railway and Railway board. In his railway budget speech, Mr. Suresh Prabhu has announced that "We are setting aside a sum of Rs. 50 crore for providing innovation grants to employees, startups, and growth-oriented small businesses to support internal and external innovation. On an annual basis, we will seek out solutions to IR's most critical problems through an Innovation Challenge. The initiative would be administered by an Innovation Committee comprising reputed investors, representatives from the National Academy of Indian Railways, Railway Board and 'Kayakalp' headed by Ratan Tata".

The railway will set up innovation labs in workshops and production units to support creative innovation by locals and staff. . Railway Ministry will set up a Test Track for expeditious testing of prototypes under varying test conditions. Earlier such testing used to perform on the Railway network, which leads to traffic delays. This Test Track will prove an important step toward enhancing the R&D capability of Indian Railways [22].

Use of Solar Power in Railway- Indian Railway Minister's vision is to transform Indian Railways, the biggest single user of energy into the biggest producer of solar power in the country. The Railways has decided to use its rooftops and land both for solar power generation. Using PPP model railway will set up solar power plants on its land and the solar panel will be installed on its rooftops. Railways will also install solar-powered sensors near bridges to monitor the rising water level during the rainy season to prevent any mishap. The radar will sense the water levels at regular intervals and send information to the central server [23].

Innovative Trains- This year Railway Minister Mr. Suresh Prabhu has announced four new innovative trains [24]:

Antyodaya Express- long-distance, unreserved, superfast train service to run on the dense routes.

Humsafar Express- fully air-conditioned, third AC service with operational services for meals.

Tejas- will run at of 130kmph and offer world-class on board services

Uday express- Overnight double-decker train with 40% more carrying capacity.

These trains are equipped with the latest technology and innovative solutions to cater growing demand for services.

Mobile App for Paperless Ticket- Indian railway has launched a mobile application for paperless unreserved tickets. Developed by Centre for Railway Information Systems (CRIS) "utsonmobile" – the paperless unreserved ticketing feature in mobile application aims to eliminate the need for printing of unreserved tickets. The capacity of online e-ticketing system is also enhanced, now this system can book 2000tickets per min and can handle 1.2 lakh, concurrent users.

The government has also initiated the process of introducing Wi-Fi services at railway stations. Indian Railway and Google have partnered for project 'Nilgiri' under this Google will provide Wi-Fi services at 100 stations this year and at 400 more stations in the next 2 years.

Twitter and Railway- Indian Railway ministry has adopted an innovative approach to manage customer experience. These days Indian Railway is helping the needy citizens reaching out through Twitter. If a passenger is facing some difficulty during his journey in Rail, he/she tweets railway ministry and receives a prompt response from railway administration. We have heard a number of such incidents like…A man traveling with his unwell father received extraordinary help when his train stopped at his destination in Rajasthan. He had tweeted asking for a wheelchair and assistance to take his father out of the train during a short halt at Merta Road station. Mr. Jain, a businessman, found the station master, a few porters and railway staff waiting with a wheelchair when the train arrived. A senior railway ministry official said the staff responded immediately to Mr. Jain's tweet and escorted him and his father out of the railway station. A woman passenger being harassed on a train in Maharashtra got an instant response to her tweet asking the railway minister for help. Namrata Mahajan had sent an SOS to the twitter handle of Suresh Prabhu. "@RailMinIndia plz help in train no 18030. One male passenger harassing me at Shegaon. I am in train and terrified," she tweeted. Ms. Mahajan had not given details of the train she was traveling in. The ministry tweeted back asking for her train details and seat number. As the train reached Bhusaval station 40 minutes after Ms. Mahajan's tweet, she found personnel of the Railway Protection Force waiting for her. The alleged harasser was shifted to another coach [25]. Such incidents show that how a government service can get improved with the help of digital and social media platform, I would say railway ministry has set an example of 'innovation in administration'.

Startup India- Indian Prime Minister Mr. Narendra Modi in his first Independence Day Speech shared the idea of "Startup India, Standup India", to encourage culture of innovation and to promote entrepreneurship. In the month of January 2016, government launched this as a full-fledged programme called 'Startup India', on this occasion Prime Minister unveiled the highlights of the Start-up Action Plan. He said "a dedicated Start-up fund worth Rs. 10,000 crore will be created for funding of Start-ups." Under this program government has offered several incentives to Startups like:

--No Income tax on profits for 3 years.

--No inspection for first 3 years.

--Exemption from capital gains tax on personal property sold to invest in Startup.

--80% rebate in patent filing fee.

--Self- Certification compliance.

--Mobile App for startup registration in one day.

--500 tinkering labs.

--35 public-private incubators.

--31 innovation centers at the national institute.

--Credit guarantee scheme for loans.

--5 new bio-clusters, 50 new bio-incubators, 7 new research parks, 150 technology transfer offices and 20 bios connect offices will be established.

--Patent regime and IPR to be simplified.

--Bankruptcy Bill 2015- 90 days to exit the business.

Besides these, the government of India will organize different events to promote entrepreneurship like Startup fest, annual incubator grand challenge, Innovation focused program for school students to target school kids with an outreach to 10 lakh innovations from 5 lakh schools. A Grand Challenge Program (National Initiative for Developing and Harnessing Innovations) to support and award INR10 lakhs to 20 student innovations from Innovation and Entrepreneurship Development Centres. Uchhattar Avishkar Yojana has assigned INR 250 Cr per annum towards fostering 'very high quality' research amongst IIT students.

The government has also launched Atal Innovation Mission (AIM), an Innovation Promotion Platform that comprises academics, entrepreneurs, and researchers to foster a culture of innovation and R&D in India. (Source of facts: Wikipedia and Government's official websites)

In the union budget 2016-17, the government of India has taken several initiatives to foster entrepreneurship and for ease of doing business in India. Major highlights are:

--For manufacturing firms corporate tax rate has reduced from 30 to 25 per cent.

--For companies with turnover less than 5 crores corporate tax rate will be 29 percent.

--Startups will get 100 per cent tax exemption for first three years.

-- For first three years, the Government will pay EPF contribution (employer's contribution) of 8.33 per cent for all new employees.

--Amendment in Companies Act, 2013 for speedy and hassle-free registration.

--Capital gains shall not be taxed on investments in regulated fund of funds for startups.

--Government will set up startup hub to support and escalate Scheduled Caste/Scheduled Tribe entrepreneurs.

--Lowered Long-term capital gains for unlisted firms from three to two years.

-- For SC/ST and women entrepreneurs Rs 500 crore is announced under Startup India scheme.

Digital India- Digital India is an ambitious program of the government of India, it's a $1 trillion business opportunity. Transparency and accessibility are the key elements of Good Governance. Digital India program's theme is based on the idea of providing good and effective governance through E-Governance. As per its official definition, "Digital India is a program to prepare India for a knowledge future. In order to transform the entire ecosystem of public services through the use of information technology, the Government of India has launched the Digital India program with the vision to transform India into a digitally empowered society and knowledge economy". I have written a book **"Dream of a Digital India-2014-15"**, it is available on Smashwords, in this book I have covered different aspects of Digital India to help you in understanding the pace and direction in which Digital India program is moving.

India a bright spot- Economic Survey 2015-16- India under its current leadership is emerging as a fastest growing economy, despite global economic slowdown India has attained a 7.6% growth rate, Foreign exchange reserves touched the highest ever level of about 350 billion US dollars. Let's take a look at some highlights [26]:

According to the survey Indian economy has emerged as a fastest growing economy with a high growth rate of over 7 percent. The manufacturing sector has been a major contributor to this high growth rate. Industrial Sector's growth rate that includes manufacturing, mining, electricity and construction is increased from 5.0 2013-14 to 5.9 per cent during 2014-15, and according to advance estimates of national income 2015-16, it is estimated to be 7.3 percent with manufacturing sector growing at 9.5 per cent.

The country has more than 19000 technology-enabled startups, led by consumer internet and financial services startups. The report said. "Indian startups raised $3.5 billion in funding in the first half of 2015, and the number of active investors in India increased from 220 in 2014 to 490 in 2015. As of December 2015, eight Indian startups belonged to the 'Unicorn' club (ventures that are valued at $1 billion and upwards)" [27].

Micro, Small, and Medium Enterprises (MSME) have a contribution of 37.5 percent to the country's GDP, there are 3.6 crore MSME units that employ 8.05 crore people. Indian government has undertaken new initiatives to boost MSME sector like Udyog Aadhar Memorandum (UAM) scheme, India MSME Communication Programme' (IMCP), Employment Exchange for Industries for prospective job seekers and employers and Scheme for Promoting Innovation and Rural Entrepreneurs (ASPIRE) to promote start- ups for innovation and entrepreneurship in rural and agriculture- based industry.

After the launch of Make in India initiative in September 2014, there is a 40% increase in FDI inflows during October 2014- June 2015. The government has undertaken several initiative to liberalize and simplify FDI policies, 100 % FDI is allowed in all sectors except Space (74%), Defense (49%) and News Media (26%). A number of sectors like construction, broadcasting, civil aviation, plantation, trading, private sector banking, satellite establishment and operation and credit information companies etc. have been liberalized.

In the Global Competitive Index of World Economic Forum, India has taken a 16 rank jump, it is now rank 55 among 140 economies.

During 2014-15, electricity generation exceeded the target. Against the target of 1023 BU, the achievement was 1048.4 BU, registering y-o-y growth of 8.4 per cent. In 2015 annual power generation crossed 1 trillion units. As per the survey against the capacity addition target of 20037.1 MW set for 2015-16, 11,226 MW has been added till December 31, 2015. The cumulative capacity addition during the 12th Plan, as on December 31, 2015, is 72,240 MW which constitutes 81.6 per cent of the plan target. Government has taken several policy initiatives to increase power generation and to strengthen transmission and distribution like Ujwal DISCOM Assurance Yojana (UDAY), Deen Dayal Upadhyaya Gram Jyoti Yojana (DDUGJY), Integrated Power Development Scheme (IPDS), Domestic Efficient Lighting Program (DELP), National Tariff Policy 2016 and National Smart Grid Mission.

India is graduating from Megawatts to Gigawatts in clean renewable energy generation. The government launched Surya Mitra Schemes and a number of projects under National Solar Mission for solar cities, solar parks and promoting the production and use of solar rooftops, solar pumps, and other solar equipment.

Concerning Road sector, the Survey mentioned that the government approved the scheme for the development of about 1177 kilometers of national highways and 4276 kilometers of state road in Left Wing Extremism affected areas as a special project with an estimated cost of about of Rs 7300 crore. Apart from this, Bharatmala Programme, an umbrella scheme is proposed at an estimated cost of 2,67, 200 crores. The program is targeted for completion by 2022.

One of the key drivers of economic development is telecom sector and its growth is quite encouraging. Approximately 33.4 million new telephone connections have been provided during April – October 2015. Under Bharat Net Project 1,03, 643 Km of pipes and 79, 994 km of optical fiber cables (OFC) has been laid up to 30th November 2015.

The government has launched a Smart Cities Mission to improve the quality of life of people and to provide a world-class infrastructure to Businesses. The government of India has a vision of developing 100 smart cities as satellite towns of larger cities and by modernizing the existing mid-sized cities. The 100 potential smart cities were nominated by all the states and union territories based on Stage 1 criteria, prepared smart city plans which were evaluated in stage 2 of the competition for prioritizing cities for financing. In the first round of this stage, 20 top scorers were chosen for financing during 2015-16. The remaining will be asked to make up the deficiencies identified by the Apex Committee in the Ministry of Urban Development for participation in the next two rounds of competition. 40

cities each will be selected for financing during the next rounds of competition.
(Source: Wikipedia)

In addition to above, new initiatives like Swachh Bharat Mission, National Heritage City Development and Augmentation Yojana (HRIDAY), Atal Mission for Rejuvenation and Urban Transformation (AMRUT) have been launched to improve infrastructure [26].

Prime Minister Shri Narendra Modi used to say "Will do everything possible to make India innovation hub." India is a young country, the leadership of the country is encouraging the entrepreneurial spirit of the people and it is leading in a right direction.

About the Author:

Devsena Mishra is an IT professional and director of DappsTech, she has good experience in different domains. She promotes advanced technologies and Indian startup ecosystem through her portal a2zstartup.com.

Devsena is Six Sigma Black Belt and Lean Certified. She has earned other credentials too, Certified Scrum Developer, Certified Scrum Product Owner, Certified Scrum Master, PRINCE2 practitioner, ITIL and some 29 international certificates in different technologies (Java/Oracle/Microsoft/SAS).

Devsena belongs to a socially responsible family of Delhi, her mother Dr. Annapurna Mishra is a senior leader of Bhartiya Janta Party (BJP) and ex-mayor of Delhi and father Prof. Rameshwar Prasad Mishra is RSS (Rashtriya Swayamsevak Sangh) Scholar. She is the youngest member of the family, her elder sister Dr. Gargi Mishra is a geologist. Devsena promotes government programmes like Digital India, Make in India and StartupIndia through her articles and books.

References

[1] D. TERDIMAN, "Technology: Fast Company," 28 Jan 2016. [Online]. Available:
http://www.fastcompany.com/3056018/exclusive-inside-facebooks-ai-hackathon. [Accessed 2 March 2016].

[2] "Wikipedia: Innovation Economics," Wikipedia.org, [Online]. Available:
https://en.wikipedia.org/wiki/Innovation_economics. [Accessed 9 Feb 2016].

[3] "The Office of the Chief Scientist - An Overview: moit.gov.il," [Online]. Available:
http://www.moit.gov.il/NR/rdonlyres/CD3AF19B-2619-415B-B2F4-B747101C5202/0/TheIntellectualCapital3550.pdf.
[Accessed 21 Feb 2016].

[4] A. K. Leichman, "12 top ways Israel feeds the world: israel21c.org," 10 May 2012. [Online]. Available:
http://www.israel21c.org/the-top-12-ways-israel-feeds-the-world/. [Accessed 21 Feb 2016].

[5] idfblog.com, "Blog: idfblog.com," 20 April 2014. [Online]. Available: https://www.idfblog.com/blog/2014/04/20/5-
innovative-weapons-idf-offer-can-tell/. [Accessed 2 March 2016].

[6] T. Rogoway, "Israel's Newest And Most Advanced Submarine Is Their Last Line Of Nuclear Deterrence,"
foxtrotalpha.jalopnik.com, 13 Jan 2016.

[7] A. K. Leichman, "20 top tech inventions born of conflict," *israel21c.org,* 7 Aug 2014.

[8] "Science & Technology: Jewish Virtual Library," [Online]. Available:
http://www.jewishvirtuallibrary.org/jsource/Economy/eco4.html. [Accessed 2 March 2016].

[9] D. SHAMAH, "65 years on, Israel is top choice for tech by multinationals," *The Times of Israel,* 16 April 2013.

[10] E. Paz-Frankel, "Meet The Winners: The Coolest Israeli Startups And Innovations Of 2015," *nocamels.com,* 30 Dec 2015.

[11] P. Suciu, "Why Israel dominates in cyber security," *Fortune,* 1 Sep 2015.

[12] J. Hiner, "How Israel is rewriting the future of cybersecurity and creating the next Silicon Valley".*TechRepublic.*

[13] A. Fiano, "Global Finance Names The World's Best Foreign Exchange Providers 2016," *gfmag.com,* 12 Nov 2015.

[14] "2014 AM Survey Report: mas.gov.sg," 2014. [Online]. Available:
http://www.mas.gov.sg/~/media/MAS/News%20and%20Publications/Surveys/Asset%20Management/2014%20AM%20Sur
vey%20Report.pdf. [Accessed 25 Feb 2016].

[15] REUTERS, "Singapore private bankers rattled by Asian moves to chase billions in undeclared wealth," *straitstimes.com,* 18
Aug 2015.

[16] A. Williams, "DBS ranked 8th largest private bank in Asia-Pacific," *straitstimes.com,* 16 Oct 2015.

[17] T. Lee, "6 innovative gadgets that are proudly designed in Singapore," *techinasia.com,* 8 Aug 2014.

[18] "News: thelogicalindian.com," 26 Feb 2016. [Online]. Available: http://thelogicalindian.com/news/all-you-need-to-know-
about-national-rurban-mission/. [Accessed 28 Feb 2016].

[19] R. Ramesh, "Business: thealternative.in," 14 Sep 2015. [Online]. Available: http://www.thealternative.in/business/10-technological-innovations-revolutionizing-indian-agriculture/. [Accessed 28 Feb 2016].

[20] S. NIDHI, "PM Modi's 'Make in India' turns one: All you need to know about the initiative," *DNAINDIA,* 25 Sep 2015.

[21] PTI, "Focus on innovation: Railways to grant Rs 50 crore for startups," *hindustantimes.com,* 26 Feb 2016.

[22] India Infoline News Service, "Innovation on Track! Suresh Prabhu announces SUTRA to support internal and external innovation committee," *indiainfoline.com,* 25 Feb 2016.

[23] PTI, "Railways to install sensors near bridges to monitor water," *business-standard.com,* 2 Feb 2016.

[24] Economictimes.com, "Rail Budget 2016: Prabhu announces innovative new trains; boost for unreserved travel," *economictimes.indiatimes.com,* 25 Feb 2016.

[25] indiatoday.in, "Digital India: Railway Minister helps man through Twitter yet again," *indiatoday.in,* 1 Dec 2015.

[26] India Blooms News Service, "Economic Survey reveals manufacturing sector boosts 2015-16 industrial growth," *India Blooms,* 25 Feb 2016.

[27] B. Gooptu, "Economic Survey 2016: 19,000 startups in India but exit options remain bleak," *economictimes.indiatimes.com,* 27 Feb 2016.